C000295596

Paper Tiger
An imprint of Dragon's World
Dragon's World Ltd, Limpsfield, Surrey, RH8 0DY, Great Britain

First published by Dragon's World Ltd 1994

All the illustrations in this miniature edition are from
Mythopoeikon by Patrick Woodroffe published by
Dragon's World Ltd

The catalogue record for this book is available from the British
Library

ISBN 1 85028 272 2

Editor: Julie Davis
Designer: Megra Mitchell
Art Director: John Strange
Editorial Director: Pippa Rubinstein

Printed in Hong Kong

PATRICK
WOODROFFE

PAPER TIGER MINIATURES

hat wonders appear when gravity is suspended and our fancy is allowed to float free.

HUNTING PARTY AT THE WORLD'S END
Oil on panel

he joy of everything
becoming what it wants
to be rather than what
it must.

THE SHIP OF ISHTAR
Acrylic gouache, ink and crayon.

hen time and space are dissolved, the underlying pattern of things can often be seen – what makes them tick and where they are heading.

haos is the birthplace of all new ideas and the muses are our guides. But they impart their insights only to those who give them due reverence.

BEHOLD THE MAN

Acrylic gouache, crayon, ink and marbling

magination and
magic have an
affinity because
both appear to defy
the common view
of what is possible.
This can lead to
misunderstanding
and persecution.

BURN WITCH BURN!
Acrylic gouache, crayon, ink and marbling

Unless the magician or artist can clearly demonstrate their case, whereupon they will be greeted with acclaim.

We all have dreams, what varies is the ability to realize them. The benchmark of art is the degree to which the artist's inner vision is accessible to others.

UNIVERSE FIVE
Acrylic gouache and crayon

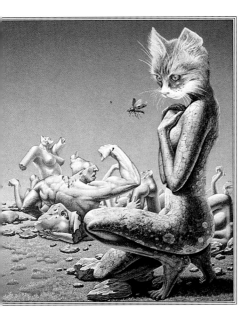

Few artists get their message across without effort, though the mark of a master is that this is how it seems. The jury of taste awards no marks for trying.

THE FACE IN THE ABYSS
Acrylic gouache, crayon, ink and marbling

 n art metaphors are made real – life truly becomes a stream whose current we trace with strange equivocal companions.

hance associations of words or ideas can take on a whole new significance.

 nd all manner of feelings which nag obscurely at our being take shape on the page with their intent made plain.

THE GLASS KEY
Acrylic gouache, ink, crayon and marbling

he highest hopes and deepest fears of childhood may pale as we mature but in some corner of our being they live on.

 n the magic mirror of imagination the world remains as full as ever of dark terrors and jewelled wonders.

THE FACE OF HEAVEN
Acrylic gouache and crayon

And in all but the most hardened cynic some trace of the child's eye remains, open to wonder and the surprise of the new.

A SONG FOR LYA
Acrylic gouache and ink

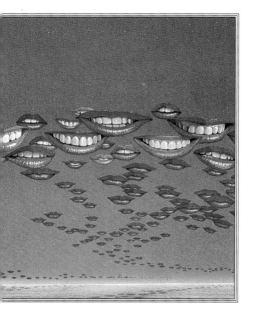

 Who can deny that this sense of openness to wonder is preferable to always looking for the worst in things?

What adult does
not recall the
freshness with
which they once
viewed each new
discovery of
childhood?

THE SUMMERHOUSE
Oil on panel

n an unforgiving
world often we
need a reminder
that it need not be
as much that way
as it is.

MUSHROOM FARM
Etching and drypoint,
tinted with watercolour and ink

nd often a bold stroke of art is enough to lift us for a while above the rut of the daily grind...

TRULLION
Acrylic gouache, crayon, ink and marbling

... long enough to remember
that there are mysteries
aplenty in life for those who
take the time to seek them out.

nd innocent joys
which cost no more
than a change of
heart, a generosity
of spirit.

NIGHTFALL
Acrylic gouache and ink

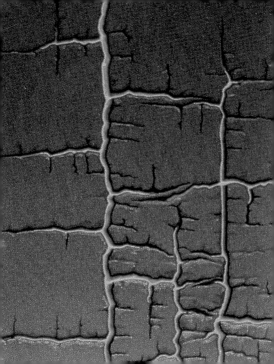